daily
PRAYER
BOOK
for Preteen Girls

Simple preteen girls prayers or everyday conversations with God

THIS BOOK BELONGS TO:

....

....

....

....

Simple preteen girl prayers for everyday conversations with God

daily PRAYER BOOK for Preteen Girls

Simple preteen girl prayers for everyday conversations with God

Don't Forget Your Free Bonus Downloads!

As our way of saying thank you, we've included in every purchase bonus gift downloads. If you've enjoyed reading this book, please consider leaving a review.

Or Scan Your Phone to open QR code

Daily Prayer Book for Preteen Girls:
Simple preteen girl prayers for everyday conversations
with God

Copyright © 2023

FAITH LABS

Contents

8

INTRODUCTION

"Trust in the Lord with all thine heart; and lean not unto thine own understanding. In all thy ways acknowledge him, and he shall direct thy paths."

Proverbs 3:5-6 (KJV)

The teenage years of any adolescent are some of the most challenging, uncertain, and trying times for any child to go through. It is the time children are tasting independence for the first time, when they start to become their own person, and when their knowledge and skills are put to the test. It is also the time when a person works on nurturing the relationships they have made from a young age, or they can even make new relationships in order to grow as a person. With meeting new people, there are also new experiences. And with new experiences, there are also new challenges and obstacles for a person to endure.

It is during these times when uncertainty and worries could tend to take hold. These worries and uncertain times could be about one's academic performance in school. It could also be in relation to someone's relationship with their classmates, friends, or loved ones. The bottom line is that it is when a child's belief could be tested the most during their young lives.

This is where this book comes to help. In this book, one can find all types of prayers for varying needs and occasions. A young preteen girl may look inside this book and find prayers for when she needs help and guidance in focusing on her studies. She may also find prayers that could help her balance working on her schoolwork and spending time with her friends and family. There are also prayers that could generally be used for any hardship a preteen girl may be facing in her young life.

The first part of this book of prayers focuses more on topics that would allow a young girl to develop her own self as a person. These are prayers that are more centered on gaining wisdom, seeking guidance, and finding their passions. These are just a few examples of how a young girl could grow into herself and become better and stronger as a person. These prayers focus more on developing the foundation a young girl would need in order to face the more varied changes in her life.

In the second part of this book of prayers, the prayers provided tackle topics that are more specified and situational. It is in this part that a young girl would find prayers asking for guidance when going through change and hardships. Also, in this part of the book, a young girl could even find prayers asking for peace of mind when going through change. One may also find a prayer that is about asking God to help them find their passions and purpose in life.

This book of prayers will help a young girl put her thoughts and feelings into words when they are in need of help. It would allow young girls to be thankful for their blessings and for the opportunities and experiences given to them that would allow them to be better people. It would also allow these girls to seek for reminders, love, and guidance.

PART 1

Prayers for Relationship with God

Prayer for Guidance

"Trust in the LORD with all thine heart; and lean not unto thine own understanding. In all thy ways acknowledge him, and he shall direct thy paths."

Proverbs 3:5-6 (KJV)

Prayer

Father, I promise I will never stop singing your praises. You are deserving of the highest praise and the highest honor. I will never miss an opportunity to spread the good news of your goodness to those I cross paths with. You are fantastic, lovely, and wonderful! In Jesus' name, amen.

*

Reflection

God deserves all praise for all he has done for us. In what ways do you glorify God in your daily life? How can you persuade others to believe in God?

Prayer for Trust

"When thou saidst, Seek ye my face; my heart said unto thee, Thy face, LORD, will I seek."

Psalm 27:8 (KJV)

Prayer

Heavenly Father, I bow before you in surrender of my Faith to You. Please allow me to trust in whatever plans you may have for my path. No matter how difficult or how challenging the path you have laid out for me may be, I beg of you to give me the strength to put my complete trust in you. Amen.

*

Reflection

In what areas of my life do I struggle to trust God? How can I cultivate a deeper sense of trust and surrender to His will?

Prayer for Gratitude

"In everything give thanks: for this is the will of God in Christ Jesus concerning you."

1 Thessalonians 5:18 (KJV)

Prayer

Dear Lord, I humbly thank you for all the blessings that you have given me. I thank you for my family, my friends, and anyone who loves me and has allowed me to love them in return. I thank you for the food on my table, the roof over my head, and the clothes on my back. Please help me appreciate all the small joys that You and life have to offer forever until the end of my days. Amen.

Reflection

What are some specific blessings in my life that I can express gratitude for today? How can I cultivate a habit of gratitude in all circumstances?

Prayer for Strength

"Thou wilt shew me the path of life: in thy presence is fullness of joy; at thy right hand there are pleasures for evermore."

Psalm 16:11 (KJV)

Prayer

O God, I would like to humbly ask for you to give me the strength to fight through challenges that come my way. Please help and guide me through hardships and pain during times of difficulty. Please give me the courage and resilience to go through the plans you have for me, no matter how difficult they may be. Amen.

Reflection

When faced with challenges, where do I often find my strength? How can I rely more on God's strength and allow Him to carry me through difficult times?

Prayer for Forgiveness

"As far as the east is from the west, so far hath he removed our transgressions from us."

Psalm 103:12 (KJV)

Prayer

Dear Lord, I would like to humbly ask for your forgiveness. I have made many mistakes in my life, and I am sure to make more of them in the future. Please help me to not allow any failures I have done to keep me down or hold me back. Please help me learn from my mistakes so that I may become a better person worthy of Your love. Amen.

*

Reflection

In what ways can I extend forgiveness to others as God has forgiven me? How can I cultivate a heart of forgiveness and reconciliation?

Prayer for Wisdom

"If any of you lack wisdom, let him ask of God, that giveth to all men liberally, and upbraideth not; and it shall be given him."

James 1:5 (KJV)

Prayer

Heavenly Father, I beg for You to grant me wisdom and strength as I face new challenges in my life. Please give me the strength and patience to think through my decisions. Please allow me these things so that I may make choices that would honor Your love and the gifts You have given me. Amen.

*

Reflection

How can I seek God's wisdom in decision-making? What steps can I take to align my thoughts, words, and actions with His wisdom?

Prayer for Peace

"And the peace of God, which passeth all understanding, shall keep your hearts and minds through Christ Jesus."

Philippians 4:7 (KJV)

Prayer

Dear Lord, please grant me the serenity and peace-of-mind that I so long for. Please allow me peace even amidst all of the hardships and trials that life has to offer. Please help to calm me so that I may not be stressed and so that I may be able to navigate through life with a calm mind. Fill me with Your peace so that I may have the strength to go through the path You have laid out for me. Amen.

✳

Reflection

What are some areas in my life where I need to experience God's peace? How can I cultivate a sense of peace by surrendering my anxieties to Him?

Prayer for Joy

"Thou wilt shew me the path of life: in thy presence is fullness of joy; at thy right hand there are pleasures for evermore."

Psalm 16:11 (KJV)

Prayer

O Dear God, I humbly pray for You to fill my heart with lightness and laughter. I humbly ask for You to grant me the strength to smile and laugh even in the face of adversity. I pray You would allow me to have happiness and joy so that my life may be a reflection of Your love. Thank You, God, for allowing me this happiness. Amen.

*

Reflection

How can I find joy in God's presence and His love for me? In what ways can I share that joy with others and be a reflection of His joy in the world?

PART 2

Prayers for Gratitude

Prayer for Thankfulness

✲

"O give thanks unto the LORD, for he is good: for his mercy endureth for ever."

Psalm 107:1 (KJV)

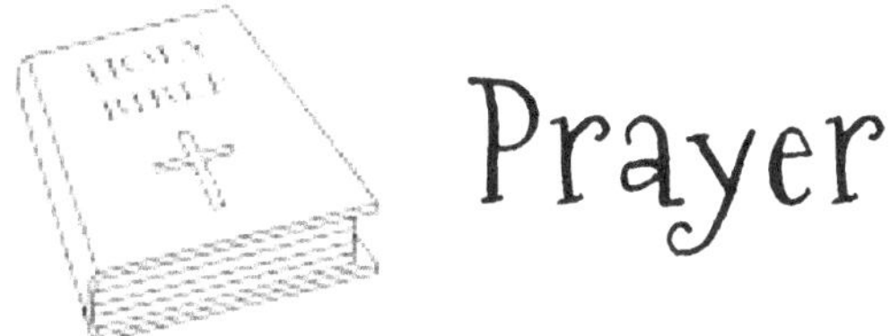

Prayer

Dear God, I humbly thank You for all of the blessings that You have given to me in my young life. I thank You for the people who love me, the food that blesses my table, the shelter I am able to sleep inside of, and the clothes that cover me. Thank You for all the blessings and joys I am able to keep in the life You have provided for me. Amen.

Reflection

What are some specific blessings I can thank God for today? What are some wonderful deeds of God that I can personally thank Him for today?

Prayer for Nature's Wonders

*

"The heavens declare the glory of God, and the firmament showeth his handiwork."

Psalm 19:1 (KJV)

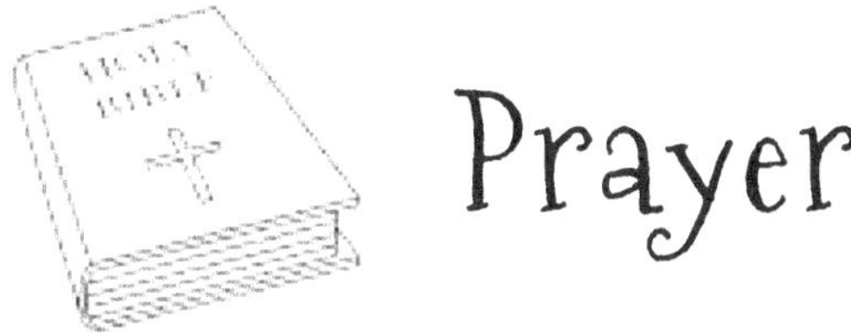

Prayer

O Dear Heavenly Father, thank You for the world You have created for me and the rest of Your children. It is because of the world You created that we are allowed to live. Thank You for the beauty we get to enjoy, and thank You for the food that is provided in this world. Please guide me so that I may be a good steward of Your creation. Amen.

✳

Reflection

How can I take time to appreciate and be in awe of God's creation? What are some specific ways I can care for and protect the natural world around me?

Prayer for Loving Relationships

"Wherefore comfort yourselves together, and edify one another, even as also ye do."

1 Thessalonians 5:11 (KJV)

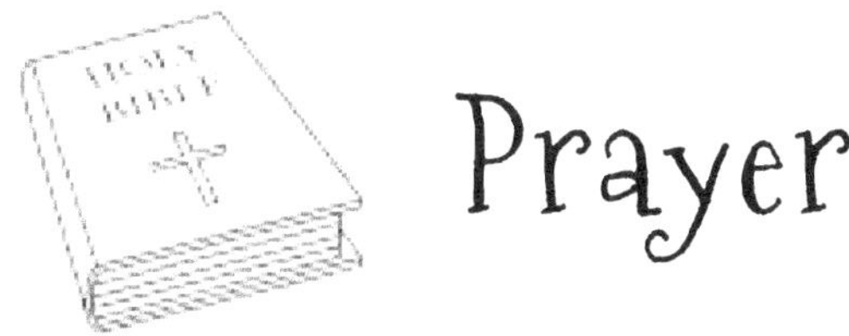

Prayer

Dear God, I humbly thank You for the relationships I have with my family and for the relationships I have made with my friends. It is only through Your guidance and Your own show of love that I am able to keep a healthy and loving relationship with all of the people around me. Please help me so that I may share the love You have shown me to the people in my life now and to those who are to come into my life in the future. Amen.

✱

Reflection

Who are the people in my life that I am most grateful for? How can I show my appreciation and build them up in love and encouragement?

Prayer for Education

"A wise man will hear, and will increase learning, and a man of understanding shall attain unto wise counsels."

Proverbs 1:5 (KJV)

# Prayer

Dear Lord, I humbly thank You for the opportunity to learn more about the world You have created for Your children. I thank You for the dutiful teachers who guide me and bestow their own knowledge on me. I thank You for the educators who work hard to ensure that I am able to learn and achieve success. Please guide me so that I may navigate through my studies diligently and effectively. Amen.

*

# Reflection

How can I approach my studies with a grateful heart, recognizing education as a gift from God? In what ways can I use my learning to make a positive impact in the world?

Prayer for Provision

"Behold the fowls of the air: for they sow not, neither do they reap, nor gather into barns; yet your heavenly Father feedeth them. Are ye not much better than they?"

Matthew 6:26 (KJV)

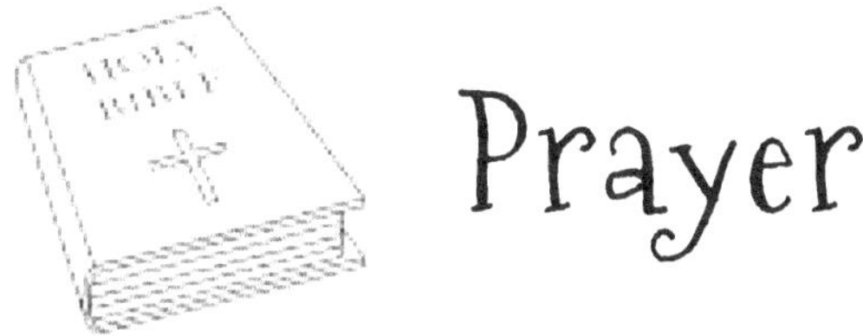

Prayer

Heavenly Father, I thank You for providing me with everything that I may possibly need in order to live in the world you have given Your children. I thank you for the food on my table, the roof over my head, and the clothes that cover me. I thank you for the people I am able to communicate with and the ability to communicate with them. Please guide me through the rest of my days so that I may never ever take the blessings You have provided me with for granted. Amen.

✳

Reflection

How can I cultivate a mindset of contentment and trust in God's provision, knowing that He cares for my needs? How can I share my blessings with others who are less fortunate?

Prayer for Talents and Abilities

*

"As every man hath received the gift, even so, minister the same one to another, as good stewards of the manifold grace of God."

1 Peter 4:10 (JKV)

# Prayer

Dear God, I humbly thank You for the unique gifts that You have bestowed upon me. I am wholly grateful for the abilities and talents that You have given me so that I may use them to provide comfort, assistance, and entertainment to those around me. Please help me use these gifts to serve others and so that I may glorify you with a joyful heart. Amen.

Reflection

What are some specific talents and abilities that God has given me? How can I use these gifts to serve others and bring glory to His name?

Prayer for Small Joys

"This is the day which the LORD hath made; we will rejoice and be glad in it."

Psalm 118:24 (KJV)

Prayer

Dear Lord, I thank You for every single thing that You have given me that provides me with joy. No matter how small or how simple, I humbly thank You for anything that is able to put a smile on my face. I thank You for the little moments that allow me to share laughter with those I love. Anything that is able to evoke joy and laughter is a gift from You. Please help me continue to appreciate these things, Lord. Amen.

Reflection

What are some simple joys and blessings in my life that I often overlook? How can I cultivate a habit of noticing and appreciating these small moments of happiness?

Prayer for Spiritual Blessings

*

"Blessed be the God and Father of our Lord Jesus Christ, who hath blessed us with all spiritual blessings in heavenly places in Christ."

Ephesians 1:3 (KJV)

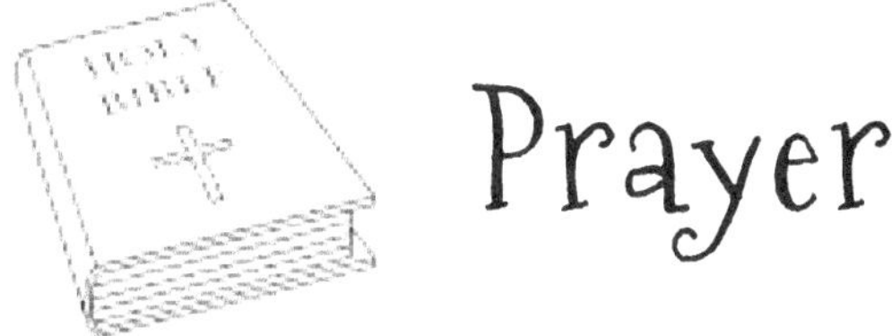

Prayer

Dear Heavenly Father, I humbly thank You for all of the spiritual blessings that You have given me. I thank You for Your love, grace, and forgiveness. Please help me so that my faith in You may grow deeper and stronger. Please help me share these blessings with the people around me and to those in need. Amen.

Reflection

How can I deepen my understanding and experience of the spiritual blessings that God has given me? In what ways can I grow closer to Him and fully embrace His grace and love?

48

PART 3

Prayers for Family and Friends

Prayer for Loving and Strong Family Bonds

✻

"Behold, how good and how pleasant it is for brethren to dwell together in unity!"

Psalm 133:1 (KJV)

Prayer

Dear God, I thank you for all of the blessings that you have given to me and my family. I thank you for the blessing of being able to live peacefully together. I thank You for the happy memories that You have given us, along with the blessing of food and shelter. I thank you for the love we get to share with each other and with You. Please guide us so that we may continue to keep loving each other in peace and harmony. Amen.

*

Reflection

How can I contribute to building a stronger bond within my family? What actions can I take to promote love, unity, and support among my family members?

Prayer for True and Lifelong Friendships

*

"A man that hath friends must shew himself friendly: and there is a friend that sticketh closer than a brother."

Proverbs 18:24 (KJV)

Prayer

Heavenly Father, I humbly thank You for the gift of friendship. I am grateful for the ability to share Your love with those close to me. I am grateful that you have brought me to people with whom I can share my values with. Please continue to help me be a supportive and loyal friend in return for the friendship and kindness my friends have shown me. Amen.

*

Reflection

What qualities do I value most in a friend? How can I develop and nurture meaningful friendships that align with my values and bring out the best in me?

Prayer for Healing Broken Relationships

✳

"And be ye kind one to another, tenderhearted, forgiving one another, even as God for Christ's sake hath forgiven you."

Ephesians 4:32 (KJV)

Prayer

Dear God, I humbly ask for Your help and guidance to repair any damage to any strained relationship I have or am yet to encounter. I beg of you to help me fix any broken relationship I have with my family and friends. Please give us the strength to keep an open mind and to communicate with each other. Amen.

*

Reflection

Is there a broken or strained relationship in my life that needs healing? How can I take steps toward forgiveness, reconciliation, and restoration in that relationship?

Prayer for Gratefulness for Supportive Family and Friends

"Therefore comfort yourselves together, and edify one another, even as also ye do."

1 Thessalonians 5:11 (KJV)

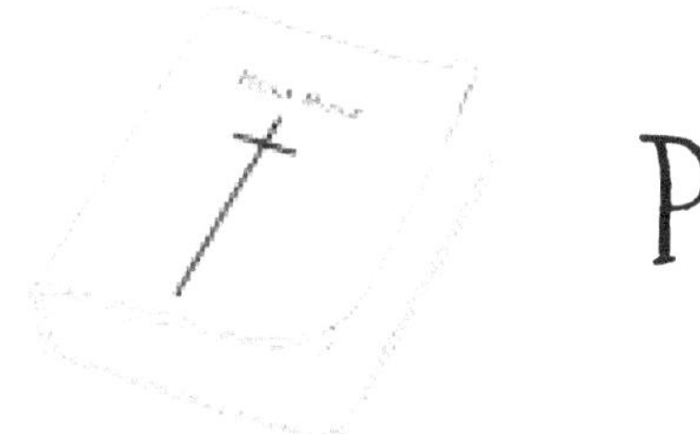

Prayer

Dear God, I humbly thank you for all of the good people in my life. Thank you for giving me people who love me and who support me. Thank you for the family who supports me and for the friends who always have my back. I pray for You to help me find ways to thank them for being there for me every single day. Please help me cherish them the same way you have cherished me. Amen.

*

Reflection

What specific qualities and actions of my family and friends am I most grateful for? How can I express my gratitude and appreciation to them more intentionally?

Prayer for Unity and Togetherness

"Be of the same mind one toward another. Mind not high things, but condescend to men of low estate. Be not wise in your own conceits."

Romans 12:16 (KJV)

Prayer

Dear God, I thank You for the people in my life. I would now like to pray for your guidance so that we may always find ways to stay together, to be united, and to continue loving each other. Please guide us in finding ways to prioritize each other and stay together. Amen.

*

Reflection

How can I contribute to creating an atmosphere of unity and togetherness within my family and among my friends? In what ways can I encourage open communication, understanding, and respect?

Prayer for Wisdom in Choosing Friends

"He that walketh with wise men shall be wise: but a companion of fools shall be destroyed."

Proverbs 13:20 (KJV)

Prayer

Dear Lord, I pray you will guide me in times when I make friends. Please allow me the wisdom needed in order to decide whether or not I would like this person to enter my life. Please give me the strength to still show them kindness and compassion no matter the decision I make. Allow me to make you proud with my actions, O Lord. Amen.

*

Reflection

What qualities should I look for in a friend that aligns with my faith and values? How can I seek wisdom and discernment in choosing friends who will positively influence my life?

Prayer for Appreciation of Family and Friends

✴

"I thank my God always on your behalf, for the grace of God which is given you by Jesus Christ."

1 Corinthians 1:4 (KJV)

 # Prayer

Dear Lord, I humbly thank you for the people in my life. Thank you for the family that loves and supports me. Thank you for the friends who are loyal to and love me. I pray that you give me the inspiration and strength to continue to show them ways of my appreciation for them. Thank you for leading me to them, Lord. Amen.

*

 # Reflection

How can I cultivate a heart of gratitude for my family and friends on a daily basis? How can I actively show my appreciation for their presence and support in my life?

Prayer of Thanks for God's Grace

*

Being confident of this very thing, that he which hath begun a good work in you will perform it until the day of Jesus Christ.

Philippians 1:6

Prayer

God, you have promised to be with me even in the midst of my despair. I appreciate your faith in me and your refusal to abandon the excellent work you began in me. Whenever I feel like I have nowhere else to turn, I am shown grace and compassion. Grace is so freely given in you, Jesus, and I am grateful that it is impossible for me to lose or earn it back. Amen.

✳

Reflection

God will still love and forgive us despite our transgressions. What do you do when someone hurts you? Do you think everyone deserves to be forgiven, and if so, why?

PART 4

Prayers for Academic Success and Development

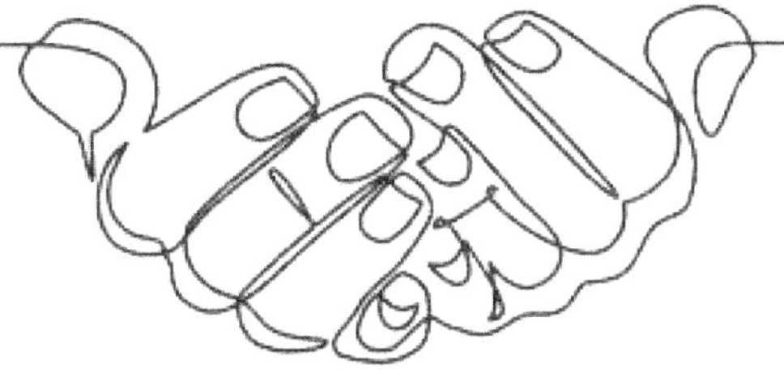

Prayer for Wisdom and Understanding

"For the LORD giveth wisdom: out of his mouth cometh knowledge and understanding."

Proverbs 2:6 (KJV)

Prayer

Dear Lord, I am humbly asking you for the wisdom and understanding that I would need in order to successfully pursue my education. I would like to ask you for clarity of mind, attentiveness, and focus so that I may stick to my studies in order to achieve the success I desire. Help me to reach my goals so that I may do you proud. Amen.

Reflection

How can I actively seek wisdom and understanding in my studies? What steps can I take to cultivate a learning mindset and pursue knowledge with a heart open to God's guidance?

Prayer for Diligence and Perseverance

*

"I can do all things through Christ which strengthen me."

Philippians 4:13 (KJV)

Prayer

O Dear God, I humbly ask for you to give me the strength to be diligent and persevere in my studies. Please give me the strength I need to endure the challenges, difficulties, and trials that all come my way. Please give me the mental strength to focus on my goals and to stay strong so that I may stay committed to my educational goals. Amen.

Reflection

What challenges or obstacles am I currently facing in my academic journey? How can I develop a mindset of perseverance and trust in God's strength to overcome those challenges?

Prayer for Time Management

✱

"So teach us to number our days, that we may apply our hearts unto wisdom."

Psalm 90:12 (KJV)

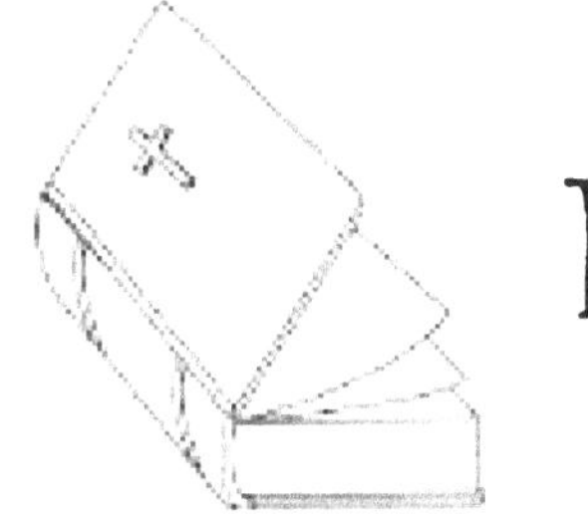

Prayer

O Dear Lord, I humbly beg you for the wisdom and discipline necessary in order to successfully manage my time between my studies, responsibilities, and activities. I humbly ask you to give me the mental fortitude to prioritize my tasks and make efficient use of my time. Please guide me in being able to balance my time between my academics and my loved ones. Amen.

*

Reflection

How effectively am I managing my time for academics, responsibilities, and other activities? How can I prioritize my tasks and create a balanced schedule that allows me to focus on my studies while also taking care of other aspects of my life?

Prayer for Confidence and Self-Esteem

"I will praise thee; for I am fearfully and wonderfully made: marvelous are thy works; and that my soul knoweth right well."

Psalm 139:14 (KJV)

Prayer

O Dear Lord, I beg you to give me confidence as I go through my academic journey. Please help me see my own abilities, strengths, and weaknesses so that I may improve on them and so that I may be able to achieve greater things. Please fill me with the courage needed to work hard and step out of my comfort zone so that I may be able to embrace all the opportunities you have planned for me. Amen.

*

Reflection

What specific qualities and strengths do I possess that I can embrace and celebrate in my academic pursuits? How can I cultivate a healthy self-image rooted in God's love and acceptance?

Prayer for Overcoming Anxiety and Stress

✱

"Be careful of nothing, but in everything by prayer and supplication with thanksgiving let your requests be made known unto God. And the peace of God, which passeth all understanding, shall keep your hearts and minds through Christ Jesus."

Philippians 4:6-7 (KJV)

Prayer

Oh, Dear God, please help me manage my anxiety when it comes to my academic standing. Please help me to manage my emotions so that I do not let them overwhelm me. Guide me through the pressure and trying times with your love and grace so that I may focus on my studies with peace of mind. Grant me the ability to cope healthily with my stress and worries. Amen.

Reflection

What are the sources of anxiety and stress in my academic life? How can I lean on God and practice trust, surrender, and gratitude to find peace amidst academic pressures?

Prayer for Guidance in Choosing the Right Path

✳

"Trust in the LORD with all thine heart; and lean not unto thine own understanding. In all thy ways acknowledge him, and he shall direct thy paths."

Proverbs 3:5-6 (KJV)

Prayer

Oh Dear God, I beg for Your guidance in being able to choose what path to take when it comes to my education. Please allow me to feel your guiding love into choosing the path that aligns with the plans You have for me. Give me the clarity and presence of mind in order to choose the best path for me to take. Please lead me to the path that you believe is best for me and for the people around me. Amen.

*

Reflection

How can I seek God's guidance in making academic decisions? What steps can I take to align my educational pursuits with God's plan for my life and utilize my talents and passions in a way that honors Him?

Prayer for Teachers and Mentors

"Give instruction to a wise man, and he will be yet wiser: teach a just man, and he will increase in learning."

Proverbs 9:9 (KJV)

Prayer

O Dear Lord, continue to guide me with your love, kindness, and patience so that I may spread these values to those around me, especially to my teachers who present me with their own love, kindness, and patience when they bestow their knowledge onto me. Help me to learn faster and work harder so that their efforts would not be put to waste. Please allow them to continue to inspire me the same way you inspire me. Amen.

*

Reflection

How have my teachers and mentors positively impacted my academic journey? How can I show gratitude and actively engage with their guidance and wisdom?

Prayer for Character Development

"He hath shown thee, O man, what is good; and what doth the LORD require of thee, but to do justly, and to love mercy, and to walk humbly with thy God?"

Micah 6:8 (KJV)

Prayer

Dear God, as I continue to grow older, wiser, and more knowledgeable, I humbly ask you to grant me the grace and ability to also grow as a person. May my character, values, and morals continue to grow and develop into ones that would honor you and your grace. Please help me grow in my personal life and in my academic life so that I may continue to serve you. Amen.

❋

Reflection

In what ways can I integrate qualities like integrity, humility, and perseverance into my academic pursuits? How can my education be an opportunity for personal growth and a reflection of God's love and values?

PART 5

Prayers for Overcoming Anxiety

Prayer for Calmness and Peace

"Be careful of nothing, but in everything by prayer and supplication with thanksgiving let your requests be made known unto God. And the peace of God, which passeth all understanding, shall keep your hearts and minds through Christ Jesus."

Philippians 4:6-7 (KJV)

Prayer

O Dear God, I humbly beg you to ease my burdens. I humbly pray that you allow me the warmth of your calming love and guidance so that my mind may be brought to peace. I beg of you to give me the guidance and strength to stay calm and collected so that my worries and anxiety will not overwhelm me. Amen.

*

Reflection

How can I actively surrender my anxious thoughts to God and trust in His promise of peace? What steps can I take to cultivate a sense of calmness and stillness in my heart?

Prayer for Trusting in God's Plan

"For I know the thoughts that I think toward you, saith the LORD, thoughts of peace, and not of evil, to give you an expected end."

Jeremiah 29:11 (KJV)

Prayer

Dear God, I humbly surrender myself to You. Please give me the strength of heart to trust in You and Your plans for me and my future. Please help me keep in mind that You only want what is best for me, even if it means having to go through challenges and hardships. I only humbly ask for you to give me the strength and faith I need. Amen.

*

Reflection

In what areas of my life am I finding it difficult to trust God's plan? How can I strengthen my faith and embrace His guidance, knowing that His plans are for my good and hope?

Prayer for Strength and Courage

"Have not I commanded thee? Be strong and of good courage; be not afraid, neither be thou dismayed: for the LORD thy God is with thee whithersoever thou goest."

Joshua 1:9 (KJV)

Prayer

O Dear Lord, as my anxieties and worries continue to grow, I humbly ask for you to give me strength and courage to push through and keep moving forward. Please fill me with Your power so that I may be able to go through these challenging times without having to be alone, knowing You are with me. Grant me the strength and courage to pursue the path you planned for me. Amen.

*

Reflection

How can I rely on God's strength to face my fears and challenges? What specific situations or areas of my life require courage, and how can I draw strength from God to overcome them?

Prayer for Letting Go of Worries

"Casting all your care upon him; for he careth for you."

1 Peter 5:7 (KJV)

Prayer

Oh, Dear God, as I continue to go through uncharted waters and new beginnings, please help me so that I may not focus on my worries. Please give me the strength and mental fortitude to keep going and to trust in myself. Allow me to have the strength and clarity of mind to push through and not mind my worries. Amen.

*

Reflection

What worries and concerns am I currently holding onto that I need to release to God? How can I actively practice surrendering my anxieties and placing my trust in His loving care?

Prayer for Finding Rest in God

*

"Come unto me, all ye that labour and are heavily laden, and I will give you rest. Take my yoke upon you, and learn of me; for I am meek and lowly in heart: and ye shall find rest unto your souls. For my yoke is easy, and my burden is light."

Matthew 11:28-30 (KJV)

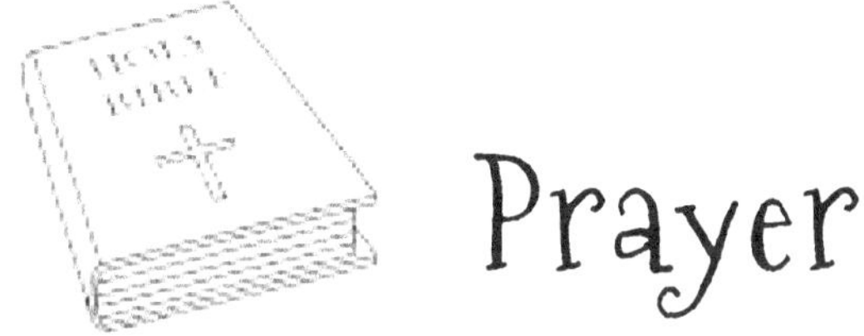

Prayer

Oh, Heavenly God, my Father, allow me to rest in your gentle love. Allow me to lie down and recharge so that I may have the strength to go through the plan that you have carefully laid out for me. Allow me to clear my mind so that my worries and anxieties are not what I focus on. Please allow me to go on to the next day or the next chapter in my life with renewed strength. Amen.

❋

Reflection

What strategies can I incorporate into my life to find rest and rejuvenation in God's presence? How can I intentionally create moments of stillness and seek His peace amidst the busyness of life?

Prayer for God's Provision and Guidance

*

"Trust in the LORD with all thine heart; and lean not unto thine own understanding. In all thy ways acknowledge him, and he shall direct thy paths."

Proverbs 3:5-6 (KJV)

Prayer

Dear God, I thank you for all of the things that you have been providing for me since the day I was brought into this world. I thank you for the food I am able to consume, the roof I am allowed to rest under, and the clothes that keep me warm. As you continue to provide for my needs, please also provide me with guidance as I go through uncertain times. Please allow me the clarity of mind and focus that is needed to make decisions that would be good for me and your plan. Amen.

Reflection

In what areas of my life do I struggle to trust that God will provide and guide me? How can I deepen my reliance on Him and actively seek His guidance in decision-making?

Prayer for Peace in the Midst of Change

*

"Fear thou not; for I am with thee: be not dismayed; for I am thy God: I will strengthen thee; yea, I will help thee; yea, I will uphold thee with the right hand of my righteousness."

Isaiah 41:10 (KJV)

Prayer

Dear God, as new changes come into my life, my anxieties start to rise as well. Please help me calm my mind and fears so that I may have the courage to face the changes and developments that are coming into my life. Please help me navigate through new transitions so that I may grow and be better as a person that is closer to the person you have in your image. Amen.

Reflection

How do I typically respond to change and uncertainty? What practices or perspectives can help me find peace and stability in God's unchanging presence, even amidst life's transitions?

Prayer for Gratitude and Joy

✳

"This is the day which the LORD hath made; we will rejoice and be glad in it."

Psalm 118:24 (KJV)

Prayer

Dear God, thank you for all of the blessings you have given me in my young life. As I achieve success and am able to constantly face new experiences that challenge me for the better, I am able to grow to be a better person and become the person you have planned for me to be. Thank You, God, for having my life in Your careful hands. Amen.

*

Reflection

How can I cultivate an attitude of gratitude and find joy in the midst of anxious thoughts? What specific blessings and moments of thanksgiving can I focus on to shift my perspective from anxiety to gratitude?

PART 6

Prayers for Finding Purpose

Prayer for Seeking God's Guidance

*

"Trust in the LORD with all thine heart; and lean not unto thine own understanding. In all thy ways acknowledge him, and he shall direct thy paths."

Proverbs 3:5-6 (KJV)

Prayer

Dear Lord, I humbly ask you to grant me focus and clarity so that I may be able to think about my future. Help me make the choices that I need to make in order for me to become a better person, be the person you have envisioned for me to be, and be on the path that you have planned for me since the beginning of time. Help me use my talents to the best of my abilities, so what you want me to be. Amen.

*

Reflection

How can I actively trust in God's guidance and seek His direction in making decisions about my future? What steps can I take to align my desires with His will for my life?

Prayer for Discovering Passions

*

"Delight thyself also in the LORD, and he shall give thee the desires of thine heart."

Psalm 37:4 (KJV)

Prayer

Dear Lord, as I grow older, my interests and talents also change and develop. As I continue to grow and change, please guide me into finding interests and activities that I would be passionate about. And once I find these passions, please grant me the ability to nurture them. Please help me figure out ways for me to use these passions to help me on the path you laid out for me. Amen.

*

Reflection

What passions and interests has God placed in my heart? How can I cultivate and explore these passions to bring glory to God and make a positive impact in the world?

Prayer for Embracing Growth and Challenges

"My brethren, count it all joy when ye fall into divers temptations; Knowing this, that the trying of your faith worketh patience. But let patience have her perfect work, that ye may be perfect and entire, wanting nothing."

James 1:2-4 (KJV)

Prayer

Dear God, change and development is hard. In line with that, I humbly ask you to grant me the bravery to embrace growth and challenges that would help me develop into a better person. Allow me to welcome new opportunities with open arms so that I may become the person you have envisioned for me to become. Amen.

✽

Reflection

In what areas of my life am I currently facing challenges or stepping outside of my comfort zone? How can I embrace these opportunities for growth and trust that God is shaping me through them?

Prayer for Using Talents for Others

*

"As every man hath received the gift, even so, minister the same one to another, as good stewards of the manifold grace of God. As every man hath received the gift, even so, minister the same one to another, as good stewards of the manifold grace of God."

1 Peter 4:10 (KJV)

Prayer

Dear Lord, the passions, talents, and interests you have given me are things that I enjoy and recognize that I have been blessed with. It is also because I know you have blessed me with these things that I know they are meant to be shared. Please give me the confidence and courage to be able to show them off to the rest of the world so that I can make the impact on the world that you have planned for me. Amen.

*

Reflection

How can I use my unique talents and gifts to serve and bless others? In what specific ways can I be intentional about using my abilities for the benefit of those around me?

Prayer for Developing a Heart of Service

✳

"For, brethren, ye have been called unto liberty; only use not liberty for an occasion to the flesh, but by love serve one another."

Galatians 5:13 (KJV)

Prayer

O Dear God, with all the strength, passion, and courage you have given me, I can only hope to pay them back in ways that would honor you. Please open my eyes to the needs of the people around me so that I may share the gifts you have given me. Please guide me so that I may develop a heart that would serve others. Amen.

＊

Reflection

How can I cultivate a heart of service and compassion for others? What areas of need or opportunities for service do I notice around me, and how can I actively respond with love and kindness?

Prayer for Trusting God's Timing

*

"He hath made everything beautiful in his time: also he hath set the world in their heart so that no man can find out the work that God maketh from the beginning to the end."

Ecclesiastes 3:11 (KJV)

Prayer

Dear God, I am constantly reminding myself that You have a plan for me. Along with that plan is when things will happen for me. Please grant me the patience and security to keep reminding myself that the things I would like to happen in my life will happen in the time you intend for them to be. Remind me that You have a plan for me and that I should trust you. Amen.

*

Reflection

In what areas of my life am I struggling to trust God's timing? How can I cultivate patience and contentment, knowing that God has a perfect plan for me and will reveal it in His time?

Prayer for Strength During Times of Doubt

"I will praise thee; for I am fearfully and wonderfully made: marvelous are thy works; and that my soul knoweth right well."

Psalm 139:14 (KJV)

Prayer

Dear God, in times of challenges and hardship, I doubt my own capabilities. In times of uncertainty, I question my life's purpose. Please, God, I beg you, help me remember that I am who I am meant to be because You were the one who made me. Please remind me that You are there for me to grant me Your grace and guiding presence. Amen.

*

Reflection

When I doubt my abilities and purpose, how can I remind myself of the truth that I am fearfully and wonderfully made by God? How can I nurture self-confidence and rely on His strength in moments of doubt?

Prayer for Living A Life of Impact

*

"Let your light so shine before men, that they may see your good works, and glorify your Father which is in heaven."

Matthew 5:16 (KJV)

Prayer

Dear God, allow me to give an impact on the world as a way of saying thank you for all the blessings you have given me. Please allow me the opportunity to use the talents and passions You have granted me to impact the world in the way You have intended for me to do so. Please give me the strength, confidence, and courage in order to complete this task as a way of honoring you and your kindness and mercy. Amen.

*

Reflection

What practical steps can I take to let my light shine before others and make a positive impact on the world? How can I actively seek opportunities to glorify God through my actions and deeds?

Encouragement to Continue Praying

"Let no man despise thy youth; but be thou an example of the believers, in word, in conversation, in charity, in spirit, in faith, in purity."

1 Timothy 4:12 (KJV)

The teenage years are a trying time for anyone. It is the time when young people would be unsure of themselves, confused about what is right and wrong in the eyes of God and everyone around them, and afraid to even try to step out of their comfort zones and take on new challenges, even if they are opportunities to become better people. However, with prayer and faith, one might be able to change their own mindset just by simply being able to communicate and connect with their God.

In the book, a teenager may find many prayers in regards to finding their faith, trusting the Lord, asking for the abilities and skills that they believe to be needed in order to succeed in their academic goals, and helping them go through times of trouble in any type of relationship they have, whether it be with their family, their friends, or even their classmates. A young girl can go through many types of problems. Some might not be going through the same problems specifically, but it does not change the fact that these young girls are seeking help in any way, shape, or form.

This book of prayers features many prayers that ask for guidance, trust, strength, and courage. This is because, though the problems, challenges, and experiences that a person goes through are all widely different, most of those problems are usually tackled with the help of being guided, trusting in god, and having strength and courage, whether it be mentally or physically.

This book of prayers not only has prayers that ask for favors from the Lord, but it also has prayers that would thank Him as well. There are prayers in this book to help young girls show gratitude to their God, their family, and their friends for being there for them, for helping them, and for being in their lives at all. While it is important for young girls to learn how to ask for help, it is equally important that they learn how to be thankful and show gratitude to anyone who showers them with grace and favors as well. A young girl can ask for as many talents and abilities as she wants, but it is also up to her to work on and develop them so that she may achieve the image that God had intended for her to achieve.

A young girl need not go through, use, or read every single prayer in this book. She can only look for and use the ones that she needs. However, she must also learn how to use whatever Grace she is granted for the better, for the people around her and for the people who love and care about her. She must also be the one who practices Grace after she receives them, a responsibility she must nurture, practice, and continue not only during the time she needs it or wants to use it, not only during her teenage years either but for the rest of her life.

Quiz Questions

Complete the Sentence Questions

1. Trust in the _____ with all thine heart; and lean not unto thine own understanding.

    a. Holy Spirit

    b. Lord

    c. Father

2. Let your light so shine before men, that they may see your good works, and glorify your _______ which is in heaven.

    a. Holy Spirit

    b. Lord

    c. Father

3. I will praise thee; for I am fearfully and wonderfully made: _________ are thy works; and that my soul knoweth right well.

    a. marvelous

    b. blessed

    c. holy

4. So teach us to number our days, that we may apply our hearts unto ______.

    a. mind

    b. psyche

    c. wisdom

5. Delight thyself also in the LORD, and he shall give thee the ________ of thine heart.

    a. desires

    b. wants

    c. needs

6. He hath made everything beautiful in his time: also he hath set the world in their heart so that no man can find out the work that ___ maketh from the beginning to the end..

    a. Jesus

    b. God

    c. Life

7. For, brethren, ye have been called unto liberty; only use not liberty for an occasion to the ______, but by love serve one another.

    a. flesh

    b. skin

    c. bone

8. I can do all things through ______ which strengthen me.

    a. God

    b. the Holy Spirit

    c. Christ

9. Be careful of nothing, but in everything by ______ and supplication with thanksgiving let your requests be made known unto God.

    a. prayer

    b. hope

    c. faith

10. For I know the thoughts that I think toward you, saith the LORD, thoughts of peace, and not of _____, to give you an expected end.

    a. malice

    b. bad

    c. evil

11. Give ___________ to a wise man, and he will be yet wiser: teach a just man, and he will increase in learning..

    a. direction

    b. instruction

    c. wisdom

12. Be of the same mind one toward another. Mind not high things, but condescend to men of low estate. Be not wise in your own ________.

    a. self

    b. conceits

    c. life

Quiz Answer:

1. b. Lord

2. c. Father

3. a. marvelous

4. c. wisdom

5. a. desires

6. b. God

7. a. flesh

8. c. Christ

9. a. prayer

10. c. evil

11. b. instruction

12. b. conceits

Don't Forget Your Free Bonus Downloads!

As our way of saying thank you, we've included in every purchase bonus gift downloads. If you've enjoyed reading this book, please consider leaving a review.

Or Scan Your Phone to open QR code

About Us

FaithLabs is a faith-based publisher dedicated to producing books that inspire and uplift readers.

With a focus on Christian values and principles, FaithLab's team of experienced editors work closely with authors to bring their messages of hope and faith to life. From devotional books to inspirational memoirs, FaithLabs offers a range of titles to deepen readers' spiritual journeys.

Thanks for reading,

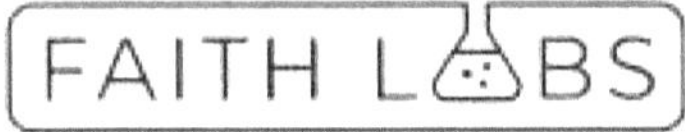